PICTORIAL DERBYSHIRE

by Crichton Porteous

Derbyshire is the heart-land of England. It is central. Imaginatively it may be written of as a heart-shaped county. A heart is the symbol of love, and it is a county beloved, by the native born, and by thousands who live around in the vast work-areas of South Lancashire, West Yorkshire, and near-by towns in Cheshire, Leicestershire, Nottinghamshire and Staffordshire.

Thus it was an obvious choice to designate a large area of the county as the nucleus of the first National Park in Britain. Called the Peak District National Park, rather more than half of its 542 square miles are in Derbyshire.

Within the county as a whole are 'samples' of practically every type of country. If a space-traveller from another planet were to land from his module at Matlock with only a few hours to look around, he could take back a very good general report of scenery and conditions throughout Britain.

In the north, Derbyshire has its 'Highlands' and 'Lake District'. Around Castleton are the 'Yorkshire Dales' and pot-hole country, with a second 'Cheddar Gorge', as from Somerset. The west side of the county can suggest Cumbrian or Northumbrian fell country. The mid-county dales are unique. South of Derby are villages and fields typical of the central plain of England; and fertile arable Lincolnshire has a sort of reflection in the rich fields encircling Melbourne.

In other ways, too, Derbyshire offers great variety of spot-samples of the rest of England. There are stone circles, ancient graves, some of the earliest crosses; old halls, mansions, and manor houses in abundance; and rare relics of the beginnings of the Industrial Revolution and of men who aided importantly England's swift rise to pre-eminent wealth and power in the nineteenth century.

Happy Derbyshire! Why, then, is it not visited by more people from the south and the farther north? Because, I think, it is too much the national habit on holiday always to want the seaside. Yet for a good country holiday, with opportunities to visit easily pleasant towns, pretty villages, and explore fascinating relics of the past; or for persons who want good walking, good climbing, good fishing, or perhaps only leisure with good food – think of Derbyshire cream on rich Bakewell pudding! – then this is your county!

(above) *Back Tor and Lose Hill, near Castleton*

(left) *The River Wye in Millers Dale*

(front cover) *The viaduct in Monsal Dale*

THE DALES AND THEIR RIVERS

Despite the great Kinder massif, which has a total of more ground about the two thousand feet contour even than the Lake District (though the highest Derbyshire point is only 2,088 feet), the most important scenic feature of the county is the dales.

Edale is wild, like a Highland glen; Hope Vale softer, more like a strath. Chee Dale is narrow and winding, girt in at places by straight-up limestone cliffs. Darley Dale by contrast is wide and domesticated. Matlock Dale is the most spectacular; Dovedale (shared with Staffordshire) the most picturesque. Very peaceful is Monsal Dale. Beresford Dale is brief, yet the most charming, though Lathkill's stream is brighter and sparkles more. Many lesser dales are all worth exploring, such as Cave Dale (from Castleton), Ravens Dale (below Cressbrook), Bradford Dale (from Alport, near Youlgrave), Monk's Dale (from Wormhill). The best parts of most of these dales can be seen only on foot. Others can be run through all the way by car.

Starting from Buxton, a good road in Ashwood Dale follows the River Wye to the foot of Topley Pike. There the river departs westward for Chee Dale, but the motorist can go up the hill, and at the top turning left descend to the Wye again at Millers Dale. Keeping at first by the stream side, the road soon has to make another climb, to Litton, but from there a narrower road plunges to the Wye again,

arriving in Cressbrook Dale. From the mill there to the top of Headstone Head (Monsal Head) is as lovely a length as any, and the view from the Head backward and into Monsal Dale is as due of praise as it was when Ruskin saw it before the Derby-Manchester viaduct was built. Now the lines are gone, and the bridge Ruskin hated has become one of Derbyshire's most photogenic relics of the Railway Age.

The so-called 'dry dales', of porous limestone, without any sizable streams, sound dull. But they are often very beautiful. Two of the most striking – Taddington Dale and Via Gellia, climbing from Cromford to Newhaven – can be comfortably seen from a car. Lovely Lathkill Dale, which is only sometimes 'dry', is exclusive to walkers.

Derbyshire has two complete rivers of note, a boast not possible for many counties. The Wye begins above Buxton and runs as romantic a course as anyone could wish all its length of fifteen miles to Rowsley, where it adds its gleaming water to the darker gritstone flow of the River Derwent.

(right) *The River Wye in Chee Dale*

(below) *Bradford Dale, near Youlgrave*

Much higher and wilder is the Derwent's source – in the peaty moors of Bleaklow and Kinder. It is first called Derwent where it ripples from Swains Head down rock ledges to Slippery Stones Bridge above the remotest of the three dams that make up the Derwent Valley complex. Just south of Bamford, the Derwent takes in the little River Noe, which starts at Edale Head and runs through Edale Vale and Hope. Below Grindleford the Derwent becomes a considerable river.

Handsome and sturdy stone bridges are among its especial attractions. Overlooking the Derwent from the east for several miles after it leaves Yorkshire Bridge is a fine escarpment – plateau cliffs, a peculiar Peakland feature – first Derwent Edge, then in sequence Millstone, Froggatt, Curbar and Baslow Edges. At Calver the Derwent gave its first assistance to cotton spinning, driving the machinery of Calver Mill in 1785. At Baslow the river passes the first of the many churches along its banks, and its first thatched cottages, rare in North Derbyshire. Below Baslow is the most ornamental of all the bridges, giving a crossing for visitors to the 'Palace of the Peak', Chatsworth House, seat of the Dukes of Devonshire. Here deer graze by the river's brink, and offer photographers a pretty chance as a herd crosses the current and then, perhaps, runs in long, agile, sinuous line up the slopes to higher pasture.

Below Chatsworth beauty and variety combine to make the Derwent as attractive a companion

(top) *Sheepwash Bridge at Ashford-in-the-Water*

(centre) *Lathkill Dale*

(right) *Conksbury Bridge on the River Lathkill*

(left) *A waterfall on the River Wye in Monsal Dale*

of a main road (the A6) as can be found anywhere. Through Derby the river is for a short way confined and shadowed by works, then flows into smooth, lush meadows for its final few miles to the River Trent, which greater river the Derwent's bounty of clean water from the limestone and gritstone hills greatly refreshes.

Of Derbyshire's half-river, the lovely Dove (the other half belongs to Staffordshire), so much has been said, what more can be added? 'Good God, how sweet are all things here!' wrote Charles Cotton of the Beresford portion of the 'magic Dove'. Yet if there had been no Derbyshire there would have been no Dove, for its start is on Axe Edge, and for its first half-mile it is a true 'Peakrill', only afterwards marking the boundary with Staffordshire.

The favourite length of the Dove is from Viator's 'wheelbarrow' pack-horse bridge at Milldale to the Stepping Stones under Thorpe Cloud, but it is a pity not to start at Hartington and walk the whole way through Beresford Dale and Wolfscote Dale, to Lode Mill, and so on downstream. Indeed, the full forty-five miles of the Dove will be found rewarding to where it, also, refreshes with its trout-water the sadly contaminated Trent.

The Lathkill, as hinted above, is one of Derbyshire's

(left) *Entrance to Dovedale*

(right) *The Lion's Head Rock, Dovedale*

(below) *Stepping Stones over the River Dove*

hide-and-seek rivers. Although it cannot challenge either the Derwent, Dove or Wye for length or volume, it is a favourite of many persons. Derbyshire novelist R. Murray Gilchrist called it the clearest of our rivers: 'A lordly pleasure for a lazy man is to rest beside the pools and to watch the stealthy glidings of the great trout between the waving weeds'. But one has to walk to see its full beauty. Although born in secret subterranean passages in a cave below Ricklow Quarry near Monyash, in dry seasons any Lathkill flow may not be found till below Over Haddon, where the fish-ponds always provide lovely pictures. From there Lathkill should be followed to pretty Alport and down to Haddon's Fillyford Bridge.

With a different, wilder beauty than the Dove, the River Goyt on the county's north-west border attracts walkers and motorists in ever-growing numbers. The stream starts in the moorland around the well-known Cat and Fiddle Inn (second highest in England), and is soon 'lost' in two reservoirs, which are nevertheless very picturesque there under the moors. Below Fernilee Reservoir the Goyt re-lives in wooded country and should be followed at least to Taxal and Whaley Bridge. Below there the Goyt joins the River Etheroe.

(above) *Ilam Rock and Pickering Tor, Dovedale*

(left) *The River Dove in Nabs Dale, showing the Doveholes*

(right) *The River Dove in Wolfscote Dale*

THE TOWNS

Small by population standards, Derbyshire towns in history and general interest can compete well with towns anywhere. Folk dwelt at the place now called Derby before the Romans came. The invaders called their camp or fort Little Chester. It was slightly north, on the other side of the Derwent, and is now a suburb. The Danes made Derby one of their chief five towns, and designated the shire. The Saxons set up a Royal Mint in Derby. In 1745 Bonnie Prince Charlie camped his Highland army in the Market Place and around, and attended a service in All Saints.

Today Derby, now a city, is most widely known as the headquarters of Rolls-Royce. The Cathedral has several notable features, the chief its beautiful tower (1527), the second tallest of its period in England. Then there is the tomb of eccentric Bess of Hardwick, erected to her own design some time before she died. The metal chancel-screen done by the local ironsmith, Robert Bakewell, is a masterpiece.

Derby is proud of its bridges notably Thomas Harrison's 18th century bridge with its rare medieval bridge Chapel of St. Mary. Now bridge and chapel have lost some of their charm, filched from them by the busy by-pass bridges which are very close. At the west end of the Riverside Gardens, Exeter Bridge with its long single span is a graceful 'back-cloth' to the flowerbeds and trees. On this bridge are four unusual medallions to famous Derby personages. The railway bridge over Friar Gate is a masterpiece of decorative ironwork.

Chesterfield, Derbyshire's second largest town, claims to be 'The Centre of Industrial England', which may lead one to expect a conurbation of mills and works. Yet it is somewhat a market town still, though in the midst of a large but scattered industrial area. The town's most publicised feature is the crooked spire of its fine church, the tallest spire in the country built of timber, and lead shingled.

(left) *Bakewell Bridge and Parish Church*   (above) *Buxton from the Town Hall*

(below) *The River Derwent in Derby showing the Council House and Cathedral in the background*

Ilkeston, although an ancient fair and market town, has grown most in the coal era. The church of St. Mary's has an elaborate stone screen, mainly thirteenth century. Alfreton, Ripley, Long Eaton and Swadlincote have also grown swiftly in recent industrial years. So has Bolsover, but this town must be visited for its castle.

Away from the east side of the county the towns are more picturesque, though Glossop, Chapel-en-le-Frith and New Mills in the north, and mid-county Belper, have been considerably enlarged by industrial works. Monyash, Tideswell, Winster and Wirksworth were much more important than now when lead-mining was profitable in the seventeenth, eighteenth and nineteenth centuries.

Duffield, Castleton, Melbourne and Repton were used by royal personages of the past. Duffield had a magnificent Norman castle, with a keep about the same size as the Tower of London, but only the foundations remain. At Castleton the keep of the twelfth century Castle of the Peak is still a prominent landmark on the cliff above Peak Cavern. The most noteworthy features at Melbourne (which also once had a castle) are the important Norman Church and the Hall, with its French-style garden overlooking Melbourne Pool. Repton claims to have been capital of the Kingdom of Mercia. Kings were buried in the

(left) *The Crescent at Buxton*

(right) *Matlock Bath in Autumn*

(below) *High Tor, Matlock Bath*

surviving Saxon crypt. The spire of the church (210 feet high) is a graceful attraction for miles around.

Buxton and the Matlocks had their heyday in the nineteenth century and early nineteen hundreds as spas when hydro treatment and the scenery drew aristocratic and other visitors even from abroad. Both places remain very good centres for exploring the north and mid parts of the county. Ashbourne and Bakewell are attractive market towns. Each has a fine old church. Ashbourne's pride is the beautiful marble of little Penelope Boothby who died in 1791. Bakewell has the tomb of Dorothy Vernon, the heiress who is said to have eloped from Haddon Hall to marry Sir John Manners.

(left) *The Market Place, Chesterfield*

(right) *Chesterfield Parish Church with its famous crooked spire*

(below) *St John's Street, Ashbourne*

HAMLETS AND VILLAGES

The list of villages and hamlets worth visiting is long. Sudbury and Ashbourne in the south have an old-world English-Midlands charm. Tissington, so close to Ashbourne, is stone-built, and yet has a pastoral air, very different from the open hill villages such as Monyash and Sparrowpit farther north. The somewhat grim look of Chapel-en-le-Frith, Hayfield, and similar villages is due in part to the grey of the gritstone of which they are built. This part of the county has become known as the Dark Peak, in contrast to the limestone area, now called the White Peak. The limestone villages have a far lighter appearance. Anyone particularly interested in the use of the different building materials should see Hartington, Hucklow, Bakewell and nearby smaller hamlets, where they will find clever and fascinating architectural combinations of gritstone, limestone and brick.

Persons romantically-minded will like Rowsley, where at the Peacock Hotel, Dorothy Vernon, the heiress of Haddon, after she had stolen from a ball at Haddon Hall and crossed the 'Sweetheart's Bridge' over the River Wye, is said to have joined her lover, John Manners, to elope on horseback. At Hathersage is the reputed grave of Little John, Robin Hood's right-hand man. The church stands high with lovely views around. At Wirksworth can be found a tablet to Elizabeth Evans, who under the name of Dinah Bede was made the heroine of George Eliot's novel, *Adam Bede,* Adam being in real life Dinah's husband. The pair had a small mill there. Swarkestone, below Derby, marks the limit reached by Bonnie Prince Charlie when he had hoped to march to London and regain the throne for the Stuarts.

Eyam has sad memories of plague, when 250 of the inhabitants died in a few months in 1665 from a bale of cloth brought from London infected by the Great Plague.

(below left) *The village of Hartington.* (far below left) *Thatched cottages at Baslow.* (below right) *The stocks and Hall at Eyam.* (far below right) *Picturesque corner of Stoney Middleton.*

The village of Hathersage

The model village of Tissington

Beside the Pool at Melbourne

Youlgrave showing the Parish Church of All Saints

GREAT HOUSES AND CASTLES

Before the Normans came Derbyshire was a playground of Anglo-Saxon kings. The Normans set apart Duffield Frith and the Forest of Peak as royal hunting grounds of boar, red deer, and all other game, and made strict laws against poaching. This kept these wide areas wild and uncultivated for more than five hundred years, until legal disafforestation was forced on Charles II in 1674. From Norman times also the Church, through various monastic orders, held thousands of Derbyshire acres for its own use and profit. These lands were largely kept intact up to the start of the Dissolution of the Monastries in 1535. Thus, in the century following, great areas of the county became available for other owners. Quickly the playground of princes and priests was transformed into a playground for gentry, until Derbyshire had more halls and manor houses than any area of similar extent in Britain.

The most ancient of the big houses is Haddon Hall, a romantic castellated manor house set above a lovely stretch of the Wye. The most famous man to live here was Sir George Vernon, father of Dorothy Vernon of the love-story. Camden wrote of him: 'For his magnificence, for his kind reception of all men and his great hospitality, (he) gained the name of 'King of the Peak''. His 'reign' lasted fifty years. Following the Vernons came the Manners to Haddon, and it is recorded that from 1660 to 1670 every year 'between 30 and 40 beeves, between 400 and 500 sheep, and eight or ten swine' were killed and eaten. That perhaps makes the Banqueting Hall and the kitchens so interesting. The huge chopping-block certainly looks to have been vastly used, and the thick-topped baking table has one of its hollows worn through.

More impressive than Haddon by size and magnificence is Chatsworth, 'The Palace of the Peak', on the other side of the hill, fronting the broader Derwent. An American has written that 'the difference between Chatsworth and Haddon is that one admires Chatsworth, but loves Haddon', which perhaps gives a clue to why the Dorothy Vernon legend has clung to Haddon so long. Chatsworth stands on the site of a house built by the famous Bess of Hardwick in the reign of Queen Elizabeth I. The first Duke

of Devonshire had that taken down, but on the far side of Chesterfield may still be visited the finest of all Bess's great houses, Hardwick Hall, a dream-place of stone and glass, now a National Trust property. Bess did not have Hardwick started until she was well into her seventies. The construction took seven years. Nevertheless she watched it all carefully, insisting on everything being done exactly as she wished, even to the great initials, E.S. (Elizabeth Shrewsbury), which stand so blatantly along the coroneted walls.

Due south of Derby near the village of Ticknall stands that undisturbed treasure house Calke Abbey, the seat of the Harpur-Crewe family. Now in the ownership of the National Trust, Calke and its fine park are open to the public. Inside are many fine rooms packed with possessions amassed by generations of the family and never discarded.

One of the most notable exhibits is the magnificent four-poster bed in pristine condition. It was discovered still in the packing case in which it was delivered to the family in the 18th century and had not been unpacked.

Kedleston Hall, mansion of the Curzons, was begun in 1759 to designs of Robert Adam, with a splendid Marble Hall 40 feet high, 67 feet long and 42 feet wide. Samuel Johnson said it would do 'for judges to sit in at the assizes'. It has great pink alabaster fluted Corinthian columns so beloved of Marquess Curzon. A visit to Kedleston, now a property of the National Trust, although Lord and Lady Scarsdale still live there, is an experience to remember.

Melbourne Hall is a very different place from Kedleston,

(from the top)

Approach to Haddon Hall from the bridge over the River Wye

North Front of Kedleston Hall

Hardwick Hall

Calke Abbey

(left) *Chatsworth House from the bridge over the River Derwent*

Sudbury Hall

Elvaston Castle

Bolsover Castle

more compact, more homely. The gardens with the enormous yew tunnels to wander through, and antique yew hedges are unique and based on the ideas of Le Nôtre, the French landscape gardener. This was formerly the home of Lord Melbourne, Queen Victoria's first Prime Minister. Melbourne Pool, overlooked from the garden wall, is lovely and peaceful. It is said to occupy the quarry from which ancient and mighty Melbourne Castle was built.

Bolsover Castle, once sadly neglected has been well restored by the Department of the Environment. Standing on the spacious terrace below the great stone front, with its double staircase from the central entrance and tall, open windows, one can imagine the glory of the days when King Charles I and his Queen were entertained here.

Sudbury Hall, now that a by-pass takes hastening traffic easily past the quaint and likeable village, is the county's only major Carolean house, with the finest suite of rooms of that period in England. The plasterwork is second to none and can be seen at its best in the Long Gallery where concerts are held in summer. There is a fine staircase, murals by Laguerre and carvings by Grinling Gibbons. Formerly the seat of Lord Vernon, Sudbury is now owned by the National Trust.

Elvaston Castle, with its woodland walks and unusual topiary gardens, is a convenient playground for Derby people. The Duke of Wellington is said to have commented on the lake: 'It is the only natural piece of artificial water that I ever saw'. At the end of the long woodland drive are the famous 'Golden Gates'.

The East Front of Melbourne Hall

The Rhododendron Gardens at Lea

Howden Reservoir – the first of the large reservoirs on the River Derwent

THE HIGH PEAK

Ever intensifying urbanisation has given many of us a constantly growing longing for peace and freedom during our leisure. That is why the National Park concept has been so valuable. The Peak District National Park – set up in 1950 – has been increasingly popular ever since, though now it is facing many problems.

The wildest parts of the Park are on the great plateaux of Kinder Scout and Bleaklow, both reaching in several places above 2000 feet. The chief gathering points for persons who wish to explore these moorlands are Edale and Hayfield, and from both, the once narrow and inviting footpaths have become in common holiday periods 'drove-roads', widening always as walkers wear off more and more vegetation at the sides. But after a mile or so, the numbers lessen rapidly, and determined walkers who keep on can still find something like solitude on remoter heights.

Still essential are stout boots, sensible clothing, a reliable compass, and a good-scale map: two-miles-to-the-inch maps which some persons still carry along, are useless

Ladybower Reservoir

The reservoir at Kinderscout

on the upper moorland amid the deep peat gulleys ('groughs' in local talk), where in any season one can get caught by sudden mists and downpours. Experienced walkers know all this, but visitors new to the area should keep to the more accessible parts.

Try the Edges first – Kinder Edge from Mill Hill to Kinder Low, which will show you the wild Downfall Gully, the deepest-falling waterfall in Peakland. Or go along Sea Edge to Fairbrook Naze, with the Snake Pass below you. If one does not want to challenge the open moor, there is from Slippery Stones, the Cut Gate over to the Flouch Inn or to Langsett Reservoirs, in Yorkshire. This is an ancient bridle-track much used before the turnpikes came in.

There are other worth-while ridge walks in the High Peak not quite on Kinder itself. One is from The Wash near Chapel-en-le-Frith, up Malcoff to the summit of Rushup Edge. Follow this to Lord's Seat, Mam Tor, and along above Edale and Hope Vale to the top of Lose Hill. Here is Peakland's first view-finder – and fine views in all directions! Some walkers claim that the best of all the ridge walks is along Derwent Edge from Winstone Lee Tor to Back Tor. Others prefer Burbage Edge farther south still overlooking the lovely Derwent Valley. Obviously the best way is to try all the ridge walks and decide for yourself.

(left) *Fernilee Reservoir in the Goyt Valley*

(right) *The Winnats Pass*

(below) *Castleton and Mam Tor – 'the Shivering Mountain'*

ANCIENT CUSTOMS

Morris Dancing at Bakewell

Derbyshire's pride is its unique custom of Well-dressing. This began in lovely Tissington, which has five wells that in times of drought have never failed, and in the Great Plague years of 1665-66 are reputed by their purity to have helped keep all persons in Tissington free from infection. Well-dressing is the villagers' way of saying: 'Thanks be to God!'

The Dressings are pictures comprised of petals, flowers, leaves, cones, berries and bark set up over the wells. From Tissington the custom has spread over the years to Barlow, Buxton, Stoney Middleton, Tideswell, Wirksworth, Youlgrave, and a number of other villages.

Elsewhere interesting and picturesque customs of different kinds can be found. Ashbourne has its Football Game on Pancake Tuesday, when anyone may take part, though it is not for the gentle. The ball is rammed solid with cork, and the 'pitch' is three miles long and as wide as the players care to make it. Castleton has its Garland Day (May 29), when a 'King' and 'Queen' go on horseback through the streets, the 'King' hidden under a big, bell-like frame of flowers, which is very different from garlands elsewhere. Original Derbyshire Garlands, used generations ago in the burial ceremonies of young unmarried girls can be found preserved at Matlock Town Church, Ashford-in-the-Water Church and Trusley Church.

At Winster can be seen Pancake Races along the main street from the Manor House to the Moot Hall; and Wirksworth and Burbage (Buxton) have Clippings, when the parishioners with linked hands sing hymns around their churches.

(back cover) *Waterfall on the River Lathkill at Alport*

Published by Derbyshire Countryside Ltd, Lodge Lane, Derby and printed in Great Britain.

Photographs by Andy Williams, Brian Lawrence, R. L. Moore, Pix Photos Ltd, Studio 71, Geoff Morgan, John Merrill, David Bowen, Roy Deeley, T. S. Wragg, S. W. Newbery, Terence Eames, G. B. Whiteman & A. L. Clayden, Vernon D. Shaw, E. A. Woodall and Jeremy Beckett.

The map, based on Ordnance Survey with the sanction of the Controller of H. M. Stationery Office, was drawn by D. G. Mackay.

ISBN 0 85100 086 X.

A well-dressing at the Town Well, Tissington

Shrovetide Football at Ashbourne